UNDERGROUND ECHOES

Nathan Lofland

FOR MAX

Go.

The trail's yours now,
even if it disappears.

(send pics)

HERE • Ink on bristol

A NOTE BEFORE YOU BEGIN

This book is about adventure, exploration, and pushing your limits—but it's important to remember that every adventure comes with its risks.

The activities discussed here, particularly caving, ropework, and other technical outdoor pursuits, can be incredibly dangerous if not done correctly. I strongly encourage you to take these risks seriously and ensure you are fully prepared, trained, and equipped before attempting anything mentioned in these pages. There's no shortcut to proper training. Knowledge is the foundation of safety.

I didn't always know what I was doing when I first set out on some of these adventures. Many of my lessons were learned the hard way. I'm sharing these stories so that you can avoid some of the mistakes I made—and so you approach the wild with the full respect and preparation it deserves. Adventure isn't just about reaching the summit or discovering the unknown; it's about doing so safely and responsibly.

This book also deals with emotionally difficult topics,
including grief, addiction, depression, and moments
of hopelessness. If you're struggling with your mental
health or substance use, please take care of yourself as
you read. When exploring the outdoors, remember that
the land is often more fragile than it appears. Respect
the terrain, the animals, and the people you encounter.

Help is available and you are not alone on
the rope. Support resources are listed at
the end, in case they're helpful.

CONTENTS

This isn't a guidebook. It's a reckoning—with loss,
with wildness, and with the quiet rope
we each climb to come back.

What follows isn't
a how-to.

It's a why.

PROLOGUE

I didn't know the fire would change me.
Not in the moment.

I was panicking—bare legs, boxers, boots—scraping dirt
with a rock to keep the forest from going up in flames.
Sparks bit my shins; smoke pulled the air thin.
But something did burn that night: arrogance,
avoidance, the lie that I had it all under control.

In trying to stop the fire, I found something smoldering
inside me too—the need to face myself.
Facing myself didn't come easily.
It meant confronting everything I'd run from,
everything I'd buried deep.
It meant no longer pretending I could
outrun the hurt, the grief, the fear.

So I started walking. Not away—but into.
Into the fire. Into the mountains.
Into silence thick enough to hear my own thoughts again.
I carried weight on purpose—food, shelter, grief, guilt.
My back ached, but something in me began to straighten.

Then I went deeper still.
I searched for openings in the earth the way I'd
started searching for openings in myself.

I bought rope. I descended. I learned. I taught.
Down wasn't where I was lost; it was where truth waited.

Underground, with the weight of the world above,
you learn that the only way out is up.
In that knowing—in the push and strain—
you begin to find light again.

When you finally surface, warmth reaches the bones,
and you know you've earned your place in the sun.

This book is made of those moments.
Moments when I almost broke.
Moments when I did.
The heavy ones I carried.
The quiet ones that reminded me I'm still here.
The dark ones, deep underground, that showed
how far I've come—and how far I still have to go.

These are the echoes I found underground.
I left them here, in case you ever need them too.

THE SMOKE

We were miles from the trailhead,
tucked into a quiet pocket of pine and granite.
I don't remember what drew my eye to the
squirrel—maybe movement, maybe boredom.
A flick of the wrist, a rock, a thud.
Fifteen. Old enough to know better.

I crouched, breath shallow, pride and
guilt mixing strange in my chest.
Dad stepped out from behind a tree, looked
down at the squirrel, then at me.
The silence that followed was louder than the thud.
"What are you going to do now?" he asked.

That was all.

No lecture. No sermon. He'd already taught us:
if you take a life, you eat it.

I stood there frozen, heart racing, gut twisted.
I could've argued—said it was small, just a squirrel,
that it didn't matter. But it did. And we both knew it.

So I said, "Eat it."

He nodded once. Turned and walked back to camp.
I skinned it awkwardly, hands clumsy with guilt.

Roasted it and chewed each bite like penance—
the meat was tough, bitter in a way that wasn't flavor.
I pretended to enjoy it. And never did it again.

They called him Lofty.
A nickname from his military days
that somehow fit even better in the woods.
He didn't need to raise his voice.
Expectations high and quiet;
lessons that stayed long after words were gone.
I thought that day was about waste and accountability.
Later I'd learn it was about reverence—
for what dies, and for where it lived.

Two years later I was on a cliff above a reservoir,
sun baking rock, seventeen and cocky.
Restless, not sober.
My friend flipped clean into the shallows; cheers echoed.

I hesitated, then slipped.

Impact—violence, breath gone, world white.
I came to next to shore, ribs screaming, friends staring.
One helped. One joked.
I drank that night instead of healing.

Later scans would show broken ribs,
cracked vertebrae, nerve damage.
But then, I only knew I'd survived.
I told myself it proved something.

College dulled the edges: graveyard shifts,
beer, classrooms without windows.
Marriage came next. Layers forming
quietly over everything wild.

A coworker invited me to the desert east of Phoenix.
February air sharp, sky wide, saguaro like watchmen.
I said yes before thinking.
My body wasn't ready.
Pain returned. The cliff in my spine still waiting.
I came home limping and let it go.

Years slid by.
I stopped showing myself.
Days became months.
Drift turned into a kind of sleep.

Then skydiving near Vegas.
Controlled chaos, rules, waivers, selfies.
Jumped tandem, last out.

For seconds: perfection.
Wind filling the suit, laughter in my throat.

Then a tug. A snap.

The horizon began to turn, slow at first,
then fast—sky, ground, sky, ground—until
the world blurred to color and sound.

My cheeks pulled back in the slipstream.
My stomach climbed into my throat.
The instructor's hands worked the lines, silent, focused.
Nothing slowed.

The canopy collapsed into a flailing knot above us,
cords thrumming like bowstrings.
Another lurch—weightless again. Freefall.
My mind went blank.
Not panic, just a widening quiet,
like the moment before sleep when everything lets go.

So this is it.
The thought came calm, almost curious.
Then a jolt—violent, saving.
The reserve chute bloomed open,
a white explosion against the blue.

We swung hard, then steadied.
The desert spread out below, bright and infinite.
Last out, first down.

The instructor was pale, trying to play it cool but clearly
rattled. As soon as my older brother landed he ran over
and slapped my back and laughed. His friend was vomiting
in the bushes. I walked away like it hadn't happened. No
big deal. No brush with death. No sudden epiphany.

I laughed. I couldn't help it.

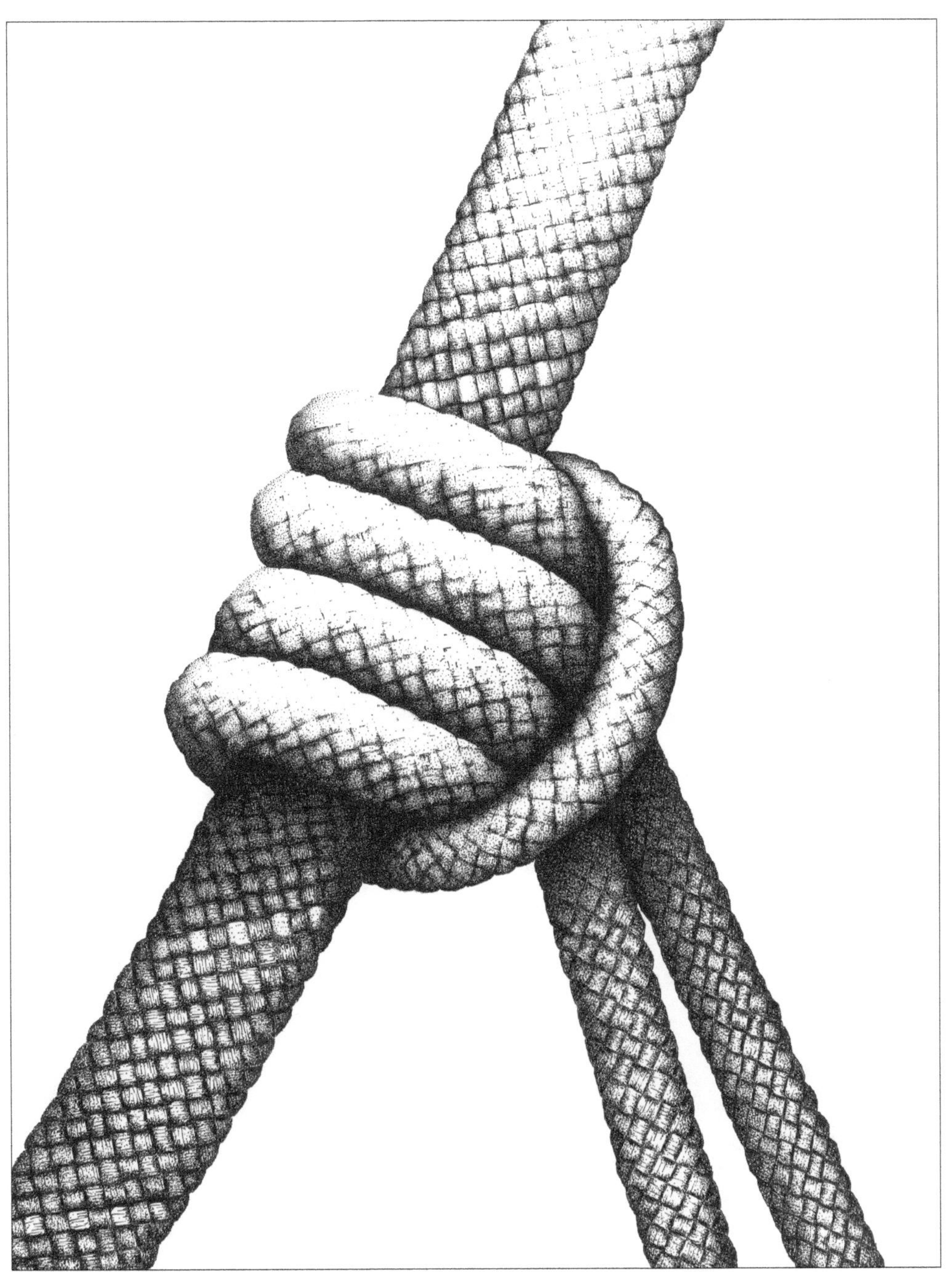

I.C.E. • Ink on bristol

We drove back to my brother's apartment, and before the
door even closed behind us, I was reaching for a drink.
No toast. No reflection. Just a blur of liquor washing
over adrenaline—numbness dressed up as celebration.

It should've changed me. It didn't.
I mistook survival for strength.
Like the cliff dive, the lesson was there,
pulsing just beneath the surface.
But I wasn't listening.
I was collecting close calls like trophies,
proof I could outrun consequence.

I'd already buried two brothers by then.
The first was fifteen when he died; I was nine.
The second was twenty-five; I was twenty-three.
Both gone suddenly, violently.
No warning. No goodbye.
No easy closure.
Just emptiness, and the quiet fear it leaves behind.

I hadn't grieved them. Not really.
I just kept moving, kept drinking,
diving headfirst into the next thing that made me feel alive.

But the cracks were widening.
And of course, my wife saw them first.

At home, I was quiet—
but not the kind that listens.

Not the comforting kind.

It was the kind that drifts past someone without looking.
The kind that forgets to ask how they're really doing.

The kind that hangs like fog—present, but hard to hold.

I missed the signs. Not because they
weren't there, but because I wasn't.

She tried, in her own way. Little signals—flickers
of disappointment, of hope, of need. But I was
too buried in my own unraveling to respond.
And she was too proud to say it plainly.

Quiet became resentment, and resentment
settled into quiet distance—on the same couch,
under the same roof, with nothing left to say.

We were both too stubborn.
She wouldn't ask me to stay.
And I wouldn't stay unless she did.
So the cracks widened.

Suddenly, the couch was gone.
The house. The routine. The illusion.

Papers filed.
Boxes loaded.
Heart packed fearfully.

Weeks later, hiking with an old friend's ex.
First trip after divorce.
Legs moving, thoughts not.
The match relit something buried,
but I wasn't ready to carry it.

The trail was beautiful.
I barely noticed.
Only the view had changed.

THE FIRE

Different trail. Same pull. I woke in the tent alone—
family camped just yards away: my youngest
brother and my nephew, both asleep.

It should've been a peaceful night in the forest.
But something felt wrong.

The air was warm—too warm for 3 a.m.—and the glow
on my tent walls wasn't moonlight. It was richer, pulsing.
I stepped outside to piss, groggy and barefoot. No pants.

That's when I turned around and saw it:
a nearby tree lit like a bonfire, sap hissing, the heat
touching my skin before the fear reached my chest.

The forest was on fire.

I stood there for a beat too long, just watching the flames
climb up a trunk like they had every right. It reminded
me of that morning with the squirrel—the same knot
in my stomach, the same sudden quiet after the kill.
Only this time, there was no single body on the ground.
Just a growing, hungry blaze I couldn't take back.

I half-expected my dad's voice behind me:

What are you going to do now?

But this wasn't something I could gut and bury. Couldn't shove it down, couldn't walk away. I had to meet it. My boots were on before the thought finished forming.

No time for pants. No need in that heat. I shook little brother's tent. "There's a fire."

He rolled over, groggy. "I know, we had one," he muttered—meaning the fire they'd made hours ago while I was out.

We'd aimed for a spring for the first night before a summit attempt, a tucked-away source I thought I knew. But when we got there, it was bone dry. I hadn't realized it was seasonal. That one misjudgment sent me backtracking miles with every bottle and bladder we had, chasing water in the heat while they stayed behind. By the time I got back—legs shaking, pack sloshing—the sun was gone, the fire was "out," and they were already zipped into their tents.

Not out enough, apparently.

"No," I said. ***"There's a fire."***

He heard it then—the edge in my voice. He bolted upright, out of the tent. My nephew followed, both of them barefoot in the dark, stunned. They just stood there at first, faces flickering, not yet grasping it. Wanting direction? Needing it?

I moved.

One. Two. Three trees on fire—two standing, one
massive trunk laying between them, fully engulfed,
feeding the others like a fuse line. Flames raced
from heartwood to canopy in a huge orange neon
U. I didn't know what to do about the trees. But
my body heard them anyway—and moved.

I stomped. Grinding out the embers already dotting
the forest floor like seeds of destruction.

Stomp. Grind. Stomp.

They followed—joining the rhythm without a word.

I grabbed a flat-edged rock and started scraping. Frantic,
hunting for something—anything—nonflammable.
Dirt. Dust. Earth. Maybe it wasn't about fixing what
I'd done. Maybe it was just about trying anyway.

Squatting. Scraping. Scooping. Twisting. Throwing.

Then stomping again. And again.
Back to the dirt. Clawing at the very
ground we'd endangered—trying to save
the place that had welcomed us.

Unsure if we could.
But we kept trying.

Hours passed—boots abused, hands torn and filthy,
sweat cutting streaks through ash-blackened faces. Fear
remained, but something else showed up too: momentum.

The ring of glowing forest floor had shrunk—ember
polka dots gone, stray branches now only smoldering.

Now, the trees stood like sentinels of our failure.
Still on fire.
Still feeding the air with their light.

And we stood there, breathless, finally
facing the next question: *What now?*

We huddled.
Smoke in our eyes. No water. No tools.
No plan. Just fear and a glowing blaze.

I said we take shifts. One sleeps, two work.
Then rotate. Over and over until it's out—or we are.

He shook his head.

"Let's go," he said. "Right now.
I'm not trying to wake up dead."

"No."

Too fast, too loud. But I meant it. I *had* to stay.
And I needed him with me.

I reminded him how hard it was getting here. The heat,
the miles, his legs cramping halfway up that hill.

"If we leave and this spreads," I said, "every hour
they spend fighting it—every drop of sweat,
every boot step up this ridge—that's on us."

He didn't say anything.

So I added, "You won't wake up dead. I'll wake you first."

He looked at me. Then nodded.
Not convinced. Just unwilling to leave without me.
He was good like that.

Later, much later, I'd think about that line.

I'll wake you first.

And how sometimes, no matter how hard you
shake someone, you can't. But not then.

Then it was scrape, throw, stomp, repeat. A plan.

Clear fuel. Throw dirt. Watch for falling branches.
Stop them from rolling and starting something
worse. One person rests. The other two work. I'd
hauled water last night. Got maybe two hours of
sleep. I was up first, so I was down first. One hour.

I kicked off my boots, crawled into the tent, and passed out as the sky began to lighten—listening to the sounds of my brother and nephew scraping at the edge of the damage.

I woke to a gray sky and the smell of smoke still thick, but quieter now. My body ached but there was no time to stretch or ease back into the work. The others were still at it, but the fire had barely budged. The big trunk still burned stubbornly, heat pouring off it in waves, the standing trees still smoldering like ancient torches.

We rotated. Stomp. Scrape. Throw. Repeat. No one spoke much. There wasn't much to say. Our drinking water was nearly gone again, and none of us had the strength or morale for another miles-long trek. We were moving like ghosts—scraped raw, bone tired, running on nothing but obligation.

The air changed first—pressure dropping, a smell like metal.

Then—a shift.

A drop hit my arm. Heavy. Real. I looked up. Another on my cheek. Then on the fire.

We froze for a beat—then exploded into motion.

TREE • Ink on bristol

We scrambled like lunatics, shoving cook pots out, yanking bottles from packs, even catching drops with our mouths like kids in a sprinkler. My brother and nephew positioned cups under their tent rainflies to catch runoff. It wasn't elegant, but it was working.

And just like that—water. Actual water.
Enough to sip. Enough to heat.

Enough to affect the fire.

Soon we were huddled under a pine bough, cradling hot coffee, still filthy and reeking of smoke and sweat. But we were *laughing*. Deep, stupid laughter that comes from being too tired to pretend anything's normal. My brother snorted hot coffee out his nose trying to describe my half-naked dirt-flinging from earlier. My nephew claimed credit for summoning the rain with sheer willpower. We gave him the win.

It was absurd—the same forest that had nearly burned us alive now gently rinsing our faces while we giggled over coffee like it was a campout gone weird. But the fire still smoldered. And we weren't done yet.

We just had a little help now. And we were grateful— not in some poetic, sit-around-and-hold-hands kind of way. But a raw, spent, primal gratitude. For water. For pause. For the chance to keep trying.

We stayed another night, soaked but steady. The
fire hissed and smoked, but it no longer raged. We
took turns poking and checking and poking again.
No more sleep rotations. No more urgency.

Just slow, persistent watching.

Making sure.

By morning, we were sure.
The flames were out. Embers drowned.
The trees—blackened skeletons now—stood silently in
the mist. Their heat gone, but their message burned in.

We packed up in silence, sore and filthy,
quieter than we'd ever been.

Just before losing sight of camp, I saw them: two upright
trees, the massive fallen trunk between them—
a giant, smoking "U."

You. You did this.
But also—
You stayed.
You tried.

I carried it long after the forest forgot.

THE FALL

I carried that "U" branded deep—
not as punishment,
but as reminder:
of what I'd burned,
of what I couldn't unsee,
of what I could no longer excuse.

I hadn't just hurt a patch of forest.
I'd scorched through people's trust,
torched my own dignity,
left a trail of ash behind—
relationships dry as tinder,
promises with blackened edges.

I scraped at my shame,
and every time, I threw it on them.
Worse, I stopped noticing.

Until that night...

There's a kind of quiet that comes after destruction.

It's not peaceful.
It's hollow.

Not an absence of noise, but an absence of care.

CRACK • Ink on bristol

It starts with a fracture. A shift.

Just a thin line where pressure finds a weakness—
wide enough for a trickle to get in.

Over time, quietly, that trickle dissolves
the stone around it.

Some rock is carried deeper by the slow flow.
Some remains—unchanged, unmoved.

What begins as a crack becomes a hollow.

An absence.
A cavern.
A cave.

That's where I lived for a while.
Not buried, but close.

I'd wake up knowing I'd hurt someone the night before—
sometimes with words, sometimes with silence.
Sometimes with nothing more than my absence.

And still, I'd find a way to justify it. To minimize it.
I wasn't drinking that much.
I still showed up.
I wasn't the worst one in the room.

But the fire burned that story down, too.

The fun, the adventure, the confidence and sense
of belonging, the cheer and joy that alcohol had
showed me earlier in life, came at a cost. And I
had signed that deal, completely uninterested in
the fine print. And it had come to collect.

Knocking. Knocking. Louder each time.

The thought came sharp and fast: not again. Not this way.

Banging. Cracking.
Splintering the door,
no matter how I'd tried to reinforce it.
It was breaking open.
And there was nothing I could do to stop it.
Nothing left standing between me and consequence.

Every single tool I had failed.

I was hanging from a ledge too small to rest on.
One I'd climbed to blindly, without thinking.
And I was giving up.
Fingers sore from scraping.
No strength left to hold on.
I was letting go.

Crashing into the bottom of my unintentional cave.

No rope. No hope. No first aid kit. No compass.
Self-inflicted wounds with nowhere to turn.

No passion for life. So much left to lose.
But no purpose.

Dizzied again by the rotating horizon.
The cavern floor rushing toward me.

I didn't care.

But something in me must have.

Some buried, hiding *part* of me broke free—just long
enough to look up at the stars, close my eyes, and
from deep, deep within let out a faintly audible:

"Help."

And just then, something new.
A message. A fluke. Coincidence. Projection.
It doesn't matter. It hit me like truth.

The air cooled on my skin.
I opened my eyes just in time to see a single
shooting star cross the darkening sky.

Calm rippled through me. My breath slowed.
My heart quieted. My muscles let go.

For the first time in a long time,
Everything was... OK.

STARS THAT NIGHT • Scratchboard

Of course, when I told my older brother
about the shooting star,
He just shrugged and said,
"Well yeah, dummy. There was a meteor shower."

And he was right.

But that didn't make it any less true.
Because it wasn't about the meteor.

In that moment, there was no reason for
me to feel peace. Or comfort.

I was void of those two things.

Yet there they were.

Not crashing in—just settling around me.
Soft. Still. Steady.
Like a blanket pulled up by unseen hands.

And they didn't promise anything.
They didn't fix anything.

But they wrapped around me with just enough strength
to make the next part possible.
To try.
To stop turning away.
To stop justifying it.
To stop ignoring it.
To face it.

To try.

Even if no one joined me.
Even if he wouldn't.

He always jumped first.
Out of planes. Into jokes. Into the room.
Older brother stuff—louder, braver, always in motion.

Maybe I needed the bottom.

Maybe he needed the wind.

The air went thin.
It felt like falling without a chute.

But that simple act, that whisper, that primal plea—
it pulled a reserve.

Not enough for a soft landing.
Just enough to survive it.

A part of me only watched, recording it all.

Sometimes I still hear his voice.
Not out loud—just tucked in the folds of memory.

"What are you going to do now?"

He asked it once, after I killed something I shouldn't.
He didn't need to say more—the silence did the rest.

That question became something else after that night.
It wasn't about a squirrel.
Not even about the flames.
It was about every time I hurt someone and walked away—
including me.

It was time to stop the steady flow
that once had been a trickle.

It was time to stop drinking.
It was time to find a rope.

THE PATH

I almost brought a bottle—nobody would know.
But I heard his voice: *What are you going to do now?*
Not in accusation. Not even out loud.
Just there, quietly, like it had been waiting.

If I brought a small bottle, I'd finish it before sundown,
hike back to town for more, and call it a trip.

If I brought a big one, I'd drink too much the first night,
wake up wrecked, and never even try for the summit.

That wasn't a guess. That was history.
So I didn't.

But I also wanted to see what would happen
if I didn't take the easy way out.

It isn't the tallest peak in Utah, not even
close. But it had been waiting.

It was the summit I hadn't reached on the fire trip—the
one I couldn't go chasing when everything was burning
behind me. That second day was meant for this summit.
Instead, I spent it scraping dirt, throwing it on flames,
stomping embers. Scrape, throw, stomp, repeat.

This time, I found a different rhythm.

Step, breathe, step, repeat.

At the top: not triumph. Stillness.
A loneliness earned by choosing my path.
No brother beside me. No celebration.
Just me—finally here—on a path only I could walk.

But even that ache carried something new. Not
relief, not pride—just the faintest sense that I'd done
something hard. That I could do something hard.

That feeling walked back down the mountain with
me. It didn't fix anything, but it gave me just enough
to do the next hard thing: ask a stranger for help.

Someone who knew exactly what I hadn't
been able to say out loud yet.

He didn't offer a map—just pointed toward the
trailhead, told me where the next one was, and
reminded me I didn't have to walk it alone.

He was frank. I could trust him to be human. But I
also needed something larger than either of us.

And the answer had been obvious all along.
I'd seen it, felt it, even heard it—often.
Sometimes I noticed. Rarely did I listen.

Really accepting that gave me freedom.
Surrendering to it released me.

And gave me hope—hope big enough to commit to trying.

There had already been a long history of trail
markers laid out for me. Not by someone.
Not by something. By everything.

By the bird calls that warned me of a stalking
cougar. By the sunlit ice sculpture deep in a cave
that lit the way so fully I didn't need my headlamp.
By the single blue rock—just wrong enough to stop
me mid-step and make me realize I'd strayed off
course. By the moose who chose to lie down and
sleep beside my tent, like I belonged there too.

That was enough. And more.

That summer, I spent whole weekends wandering
ridgelines and drainages, searching for openings in
the ground. Not mapped, not marked. I knew the
caves were out there—somewhere—but finding
them meant moving slow, watching the land like
it might whisper a secret. One breeze too cold.
One crack too sharp. One stone out of place.

Most of the time, I found nothing.

I'd climb toward a shadow I was sure held something
deep, only to find solid rock. And from up there,
I'd look back and realize I'd missed something
else—something real—just across the way.

It was slow, humbling work. I kept walking, feeling the weight of every step, and somewhere along the way— knees aching, shoulders raw—I started to understand the difference between punishment and responsibility. Between guilt and growth. Both in the work and in myself.

One cave, I walked past four weekends in a row. Never saw it. Not until the fifth, when I shifted a few steps off my usual path, looked at it with clearer eyes, and realized I'd been fifty feet away the whole time.

It didn't feel like failure. It felt like practice.

Like learning how to see what had always been there.

Like maybe I had to get lost a few times before I could notice the thing that had been waiting to be seen.

And slowly, I started doing the same thing with myself. Tracing old routes. Re-walking the choices.

Paying closer attention to the parts that didn't quite make sense—or hurt more than they really should. I wasn't ready to name it all, not yet.

But I could feel something beginning to open.

It wasn't a breakthrough. Just a breath of cool air from somewhere deep in the earth. A reminder that there was more to the journey than what I could see, feel, or control.

Like when I found Choices Cave.

I had walked right past it many times before, but one day,
something was different. The air felt cooler, the shadows
longer. I turned and saw it—tucked above a ledge, almost
hidden. The entrance was so subtle I almost missed it,
but once I saw it, I knew it had always been there.

I paused near a fallen log, brushing away needles to dig out
my camera. The smell rose with the movement—pine, wet
leaves, that soft, earthy decay that feels older than you.

Just like the cave, it's one of those things
that waits for silence. For stillness.

You only notice it when your pace matches the land.

It wasn't a grand discovery. It had been
explored before—but not by me.

And in that moment, I realized something I hadn't been
paying attention to—the land, the rock, the paths—
they don't hurry.

They don't care if I'm ready.
They don't care if I'm trying to force something to happen.

They simply are.

They hold a lesson—and they don't.
It depends on how you show up.

The cave wasn't going to offer shortcuts or easy answers,
just like I wasn't going to find them in my own struggles.
I had to meet both the cave and myself where we were—
dark, tight, uncomfortable. I couldn't rush through it.
I had to accept the narrowness, brave the dark, feel
the weight, trust the process—and inch forward.

So I crawled deeper, letting the cool air settle in—
grounding me in a way I hadn't expected. It was
just about being there. In the dark. Exploring.

It felt good to grasp a rock and pull myself forward.
To crawl low through the wet dirt, slowly twisting and
bending through mazes of fallen yet settled boulders
just to see if it kept going. Because I chose to be there.

It was in that space that I realized: integrity isn't
about fighting through, about rushing ahead.

It's about being real with where you are, about showing
up even when it's hard. It's about letting go of the
things you think you should be and simply being you.

The cave doesn't change for you,
but it allows you to change for it.
Willingness isn't about forcing yourself in;
it's about letting yourself fit into something greater—
something raw and real.

And through that, I found a quiet gratitude for my own body. I wasn't ashamed of being the runt anymore. This body, once a source of doubt, allowed me to go where others couldn't. To fit where others can't.

We won't all fit through every tunnel
before us. And that's OK.

When I finally crawled back out of that passage, there was light again. But it wasn't the same as before. I didn't need to get somewhere or finish something. I just needed to be present, to sit with the experience, and trust the next step and walk the next ridge, wherever it would take me.

It wasn't easy to let go of the urge to control,
or the desire to hide behind the mask of
someone who had it all figured out.

But it was necessary. Without that humility, I couldn't see others clearly. I couldn't give. Not really.

But something else had been growing alongside all that internal work. It didn't feel like much at the time. Just small things—photos taken on the trail. At first with my phone, nothing fancy. Just snapshots I thought my dad might like. Little glimpses of where I'd been. I started sending them to him, and I saw how much they meant.

That second Christmas after I got sober—the first
holiday past a full year—I made him a photo book.
I hadn't planned it; I just wanted to share where I'd been.
It landed perfectly.
Each year after that, the photos got better,
the books thicker.
They became our tradition—my quiet way
of taking him along.

And then, when he was dying, I had a river trip
planned. I almost didn't go. It felt wrong to leave.
But something in me trusted that he would
understand, and maybe even want me to go.

While I was out there, he worsened. I returned to
service days later to a string of frantic voicemails.
Made it back just in time for one last moment.

I sat by his bed and showed him the photos—fresh from
that trip. His face lit up. Each image drew him in, gave
him something to hold onto. He couldn't speak much, but
he was there with me. Eyes wide. Present. Regretful his
body wouldn't let him join, but somehow still alongside.

And instead of using those last moments to
be swallowed by grief, I was able to give him
something. A moment of peace. Of imagination.
A last little adventure to carry him home.

I didn't need to say all the things I thought I should have.
The words weren't the point anymore. What mattered
was the moment we shared—quiet, simple, and real.

The photos had become a natural bridge between
us—delicate, solid. A way to bring him along even
when he couldn't cross it with me. And when I said,
"I'm proud to be your son," something shifted in me. It
wasn't about validation anymore—it was about giving
him something. A piece of peace to carry beyond.

Somehow, I found I had something to give.

In that moment, I realized I wasn't keeping score anymore.
I didn't need reassurances. I didn't need redemption. I
simply wanted to do right by him. To give back to the
man who had given me so much—not in grand gestures,
but in presence. In effort. In love that had quietly grown
over time—step by step, photo by photo, trail by trail.

He didn't change for me.
But in that moment, he allowed me to show up differently.
No apology. No confession.
Just the kind of peace that speaks for itself.

I had made it right.
Not with words, but with action.

He nodded, smiled, and gave something
back I'll never forget:
"That means so much to me."

I hadn't heard his voice in a while.
It wasn't his anymore.
It had become mine.

THE ROPE

Grief is a flavor of pain that doesn't vanish—it shifts, tucking itself into corners—until one day, you feel it in your throat when least expected, witness it shooting out of your mouth toward an undeserving target, or dripping through your fingers while holding your face, trying to keep it all in.

It will come out. That's inevitable. But the pressure valve can be gently turned to prevent being surprised by a sudden explosion. Or implosion.

Descent with intention.

The intensity cannot be controlled, but the danger can be mitigated.

I didn't need saving anymore. I wasn't dangling over some abyss, waiting for a lifeline. What I needed was something I could learn. Something I could do.

Rope gave me that.

Not just a tether, but a process. A method. Knot by knot, it became a way to practice letting go— of fear, of control, of the illusion that I could make the world safe. It wasn't about escape. It was about descent. About going deeper, on purpose.

Rope taught me to grieve slowly. Deliberately. To enter dark spaces not to conquer them, but to move through them with care, purpose, and trust in what I'd built.

But before I trusted the rope, I had to trust my footing.

I figured I should learn how to use it above ground before I ever touched it underground.

I'd found a couple caves by then—gaps in the ground that I was hesitant to enter—I knew just enough to know I didn't know anything. I remembered rappelling once in Boy Scouts, but all I took from that was the adrenaline. No systems. No understanding.

So I started looking for canyons.

There was one that was supposed to be perfect for beginners—gentle, short drops, easy anchors— but my ego was still at the wheel. I didn't want practice. I wanted proof. Bragging rights.

I wanted Ego Canyon. Or thought I did.

Less-visited corner of Zion. Remote. Not much beta, no signs. The kind of canyon the park doesn't even list on its wilderness permit system—but if you ask for it by name, they'll give you a form. A checklist. Something to confirm you're ready.

We filled it out. Probably too quickly.

The ranger didn't say much. Just slid the permit across the counter with a look that said, *You sure about this?*

We weren't. But we thought we were.
That should've told us something.

But we were too dumb to be scared. Or maybe we thought the nerves were just excitement. I had two new friends eager to follow me into the unknown, fully aware of how little any of us knew. Which made it worse. I wasn't guiding them—I was performing.

We started late. Too late. None of us were in shape for the grueling approach, but hours later we stood at the rim of the canyon, staring down hundreds of vertical feet to the floor. At the first anchor, we paused—nervous, exhilarated. I was leading, knots pulled up on my phone, using the wrong rope, trying to look like I knew what I was doing.

Shockingly, the descent was fairly smooth.

Only one of us dropped his belay device from the anchor before the final 100-foot rappel. We rigged mine onto the rope, he hauled it up, and one by one we made it down. Grinning like we'd pulled something off. Like we deserved to feel proud.

But we forgot the canyon wasn't done with us.

It was June, but down there—trapped between sandstone walls four or five hundred feet tall—the sun barely reached the floor. And only for a moment. By dusk, we still hadn't exited. Still had drops to complete. We were soaked. The air was turning sharp, the kind of cold that finds your bones and then sits there. Waiting.

Our bodies were shaking. We weren't just unprepared—we were in trouble.

No dry bags. No wetsuits. No ascenders. We had carried full packs to use the campground near the exit, instead of doing the 19 mile loop in one day. That mistake slowed us with the extra weight of water-logged gear. Yet likely saved us too.

The deep orange glow of the sandstone walls began to fade as we made an illegal fire that night. Huddled in a pocket of sand beneath a scrubby bush, wrapped in wet sleeping bags and shame. We told ourselves the rangers would rather complain about a fire than a recovery.

The stars overhead didn't care what we'd done wrong. They just looked down, silent, the way they usually do.

Descent used to mean collapse. But now it meant rope. Anchor. Intention. The choice to go down, and the skills to come back up.

Now when I take someone into a cave—or to a
place I love—it's never just about the route or the
rope. It's about the bridge. That quiet connection
between people, between a person and a place.
The transfer of trust, wonder, maybe even awe.

We reached the cave mouth by late morning. A thin
crust of frost still clung to the rock where the shade
lingered. I dropped my pack near the edge and motioned
for them to do the same. They stood still for a moment,
looking down into the dark. I remembered that feeling.

I unzipped the pack and began to lay
things out. One piece at a time.

"This one's a hand ascender," I said, letting the teeth
catch a glint of sun. "It bites the rope and holds you
while you climb. One direction only. Like change."
Click.

"This is the chest ascender. Not a backup—a
partner. Keeps the progress you've earned.
Doesn't let you slide back when you're tired."
Click.

"Chest strap." I cinched it across my sternum. "So you
don't have to grip so tight the whole way. You learn where
to hold on—and where to let the system carry some of it."
Cinch.

ASCENDER • Scratchboard

I laid out headlamps next. One on the helmet, two
backups beside it. "Because shit happens. Batteries
die. And rope's no good if you can't find it."

Then: radios. One for me, one for them.
"Communication is key. Doesn't work if you're alone."
Click.

"Cows tails," I said, holding up the dual lanyards.
"Tethers that hold you when you need to
let go of one thing to reach the next."
Double click.

"Rope protector," last in line.
"You've got one way out. Protect it."

I said it out loud—mostly for them, partly for me.

The rope itself came out coiled and cool, trailing mist in
the air like breath. I let them feel its weight. Showed them
how every knot has a name, a purpose, a consequence.
How every carabiner should click like a sealed promise.

They asked questions. Sharp ones. I answered
slowly. Let them check the system themselves. Not
because I doubted the setup—but because they
needed to learn *how* to see, and *what* to trust.

This wasn't just gear. It was a new kind of toolkit. For
descent, yes—but also for the climb back out.

And in that way, it wasn't just about safety. It was about story. About rewriting collapse into something chosen.

Because descent used to mean failure.
But now, it meant *readiness*.

100 feet on rope is a workout—when your system's tuned. But when it's not? Twenty becomes a slow, grinding battle. That's where practice comes in. Tuning the system. Fitting the tools to your parts. Taking the time to pause and adjust. Because descent might be about readiness—but ascent is about return. And with the right tools, fitted and trusted, we can all resurface again.

Snowshoeing up a ridgeline, avoiding avalanche-prone slopes on either side. The pack heavy, loaded with gear for a bitter night ahead—well below freezing already. Every step measured. Fast enough to keep momentum. Slow enough to stay dry. Sweat kills out here. It freezes to your skin and drags your core temp down like an anchor. My beard had already stiffened, frozen with the rhythm of each exhale. Wind-chapped cheeks stretched tight with every breath. Each inhale sharp—cold enough to sting the lungs.

I was alone this time. On purpose.

Step by step, I moved with intention. Not because it was easier—nothing about this was easy—but because this was where resolve lives. Where restraint matters. That's where the Glacier Step became more than a method: leg straight,

WINDSCREEN • Photograph

knee locked, step, repeat. A rhythm of progress disguised as restraint. A micro-rest that whispered forward.

The goal of this trip? To feel alone.
Cold. Tired.
To make my surroundings match the part of my heart that still yearned for warmth that wasn't there.

Leg straight, knee locked, step, repeat.
The rhythm steadying what emotion couldn't.

And this time, it was my youngest brother.
The one I couldn't pull back from the edge.
Couldn't shake awake.

After Dad, I tried. I threw him lines—invited him out, showed him the path that helped me hold it together. But the bottle had him first. It grabbed him before the trailhead ever could.

His was a slow collapse, but no less violent than fire. I watched it happen like you watch an avalanche break loose—too far away to stop, too close not to feel the rumble.

Leg straight, knee locked—step, repeat.

There's no fire for you anymore, Bro. You're at rest. But something still smolders in me. And I have to keep watch— not to put it out, but to keep it from spreading.

Leg straight.
Knee locked.
Step.
Repeat.

And barely two months later, Mom was gone too.

That was the weight I'd packed for this trip. Not just
the tent, the shovel, the stove—but the grief, too.

Leg straight, knee locked. Step, repeat.
Not punishment—presence.
Stopping long enough to feel it.

To say their names in the silence.
And then—keep moving.

Somewhere in the slow crunch of snow, the fog began
to break—not the weather, but the one I'd carried. The
quiet haze that had dulled everything since the last
loss. It didn't lift all at once, but in that rhythm— leg
straight, knee locked, step, repeat—it started to thin.

I didn't realize until then how many
rhythms had carried me here.

First, on hands and knees—scraping fire-scabbed
earth with a rock, stomping down heat in panic.

Then upright, walking again—shaky, sober, sweating
grief through switchbacks. Step, breathe, step, repeat.

IMPRINT • Photograph

And now, Glacier Step. Calculated. Controlled. Every
move designed to avoid collapse and overreach.

The rhythm had changed. And with it, so had I.

This wasn't about rushing ahead.
It was about owning every inch—of the descent,
and the climb back up.
Because sometimes, the way forward *is* down.
And deeper still—in.
Not in failure, but in intention.

In caves, there's no storm above to blame.
No fire racing tree to tree.
Just gravity, silence, and the knots you tie by headlamp.

Every move becomes a question:
Do you trust this system?
Do you trust yourself?

But even in the deep, storms can find you.
The earth doesn't always shelter you from the sky.

DESCENT • Photograph

THE DEAL

The rope goes both ways.
Down through fear and up through effort.

I hang in blackness, just beneath the last ledge,
suspended by friction and nylon.

The chamber swallows my headlamp's beam
like it's nothing—a darkness bigger than sight
and richer than imagination.

The world has fallen away.
Just me now, suspended midair, drifting in slow silence.
A hundred feet still to the floor.
Two hundred already above.
The rope hums faintly with tension.
The moist air rises from below—cool, mineral, alive.

It started in daylight, with moss-covered walls and
filtered sun. Then came the silence. The narrowing.
The mud. Now I'm inside something bigger than
instinct can grasp—a cavern the size of a cathedral,
an acre of darkness much richer than memory.

There is no exit but the rope.

No one can carry you back up. You descend knowing
you *must* return on your own. That's the deal.

These were the big ones—the ones I had
dreamed about, trained for, feared.

The ones that demanded everything—and then
some—before they'd offer anything back.

The long routes. The stitched-together lines across
ridges, around lakes, down into caves so deep your
lungs and legs feel them days later. Some trips crossed
entire ranges. Some less than a mile—but vertical.

I once fell from fourteen thousand feet, when the
chute opened—and then failed. Since that fall,
I've climbed more than two hundred thousand—
halfway to space—one step at a time.

None of those climbs were easy. Each one asked for
something new—patience, precision, humility.

And that doesn't even count the rope work—
thousands of vertical feet ascended, jug by jug, in
pits and shafts or on training cliffs where every foot
had to be earned twice. Up was the only way out.

I've shouldered a large pack bloated with nothing but
water, hauled into steep, forgotten ravines to stage
for pushes no one would ever see. Edged across
bulletproof snow slopes, kicking in again and again
just to hold ground. Clawed through thorny brush
to keep from sliding down slopes that wanted to

throw me. Jumped from cliff to tree. Turned back at
the edge of reason. Pushed forward when I probably
shouldn't have. And sometimes—barely—it paid off.

Each step away from the trailhead,
I stayed—present, clear, alive.

Present.
Clear.
Alive.

I remained able to help if someone needed me.

I stayed with the hard parts, the quiet parts,
the parts that made me ache. I stayed *me*.

But staying doesn't mean pushing blindly forward.

Staying, sometimes, is standing still at the edge of a cornice
and deciding not to cross. It's the gut check that stops the
summit bid. It's turning around with someone who can't
go on, even if it costs the day. It's the patience to wait.
The humility to try again. Pride wants the glory shot. But
staying—truly staying—means knowing when to let it go.

A hard-earned trip. A long approach into Wyoming's
backcountry to attempt its most remote peak. The
kind of trek you plan for months. The kind you circle
twice on the kitchen calendar. We set off eager, thrilled
and determined to cross this peak off our bucket
lists. We were fit, fed, and optimistic. Crampons. Ice

axe. Snow anchors, rope and visions of triumph.

But day one, not far from the trailhead, the clouds
rolled in and the mountains told us they didn't care
about our plans. It rained nonstop. Night one, the rain
froze. Then snow. Everything was soaked, crusted in
ice. The route the next day wasn't bad, but our start
was much too late and our mileage was off. I was off.

As we dropped into the drainage, too late, and stopped at
the river, high with runoff where the bridge was supposed
to be, finding piles of lumber on the bank instead, I knew.

I looked at my friends and said it plain, knowing
it would hurt: "We're not gonna make it."

It didn't land well at first, but I had done the math.
We needed another day or we would inevitably rush
and risk injury. Either at the summit or on a frantic
return push to make up time. And that was if no
more storms came. Some were more convinced
than others. In the morning we turned around.

It sucked. It felt like failure. But it wasn't. Not really.

Because the real test isn't just summiting—it's what
you're willing to walk away from. Pride whispers
"push harder." Wisdom says "not this time."
Staying, it turns out, sometimes means retreat.

To trust that sometimes, it's simply not the right time.

Trust isn't built on certainty—it's built on honesty,
and what you do when things *don't* go as planned.

Like the time we were deep into an off-trail loop, two days
from civilization, and everything hurt. Wind had kept us
from crossing alpine lakes by raft, forcing detours over
miles of scrambling and deadfall. By the time we rejoined
the ghost of a trail, we were spent—hungry, irritable, on
edge. One of us suggested a shortcut that looked clean
on the map but the shortcut was a gamble. I knew it the
second we stepped off the remnants of the old trail.

It carved its own toll into our backs, legs, faces and
spirits. We pushed through thickets and marsh,
scrambled over talus, rock hopped through the drainage,
bodies ragged from days of deadfall and misfires. My
blood sugar crashed hard. I was silent, seething.

When we hit the lake shore—soggy, uneven, choked with
brush—I wanted to scream. There was no place to camp.
Instead, I just dropped my pack and stared. No words.

When he finally spoke, voice barely breaking the
silence, "You guys probably hate me right now,"
something inside me cracked open. "Yeah." I
said quietly, honestly. "For a while, I did."

It was the most honest thing I'd said all
trip. Not cruel, not loud—just true.

I added, "But I agreed to it. That's on me."

Anger used to scare me. I'd either bury it or let it poison
everything inside. But out there, tired and hungry and worn
down, I found a way to speak it without burning anyone.

Maybe that's the razor's edge. Not the risk itself, but
what you carry across it. Not silence, not rage.

Just the weight of your own voice, steady
enough to say: *this hurt, and I'm still here.*

He nodded, quiet. Then flopped into the brush—beat,
resigned, like he wanted the ground to swallow him.

I didn't. I had opened the valve and the pressure was gone.

I dropped everything but my boots and walked the
shoreline, heart still pounding. I found a dry spot, tucked
above the lake. When I came back and pointed it out,
he looked up like I'd handed him water in the desert.

He said thanks. Real thanks. And something shifted—
not in him, in me. The anger had already gone. But
what rose in its place surprised me: gratitude.

For the opportunity. For the honesty. For the moment.
For the reminder that trust is built in these raw,
vulnerable places—when things don't go as planned,
and you still choose to show up for each other.

And other times? Staying means grit.
It means finishing what you limped into.

Like the time I hiked a full circuit through the heart of
the Winds with a bum ankle. Sweetwater Pass to Cirque
of the Towers, Big Sandy to Little Sandy, back into the
quiet folds of Sweetwater Creek. Every mile a marvel—
cathedral spires, crystal lakes, elk tracks in morning
frost. I'd rolled my ankle on the second morning. Achilles
tendinitis was setting in. Every step burned, threatening
to spill over into frustration or self-pity. I stayed. Tuned
inward, listening to my body's quiet insistence: "We
can still do this." Slowed down. There was power in
that pace. Respect from the others—not just because I
made it, but because I had enough fire to keep moving.
Steady. And they did too, with injuries of their own.

That same range saw me return more than once—up
past the Green River Lakes and into the basin beneath
Squaretop. Over the headwaters, through sun-cupped
snowfields knee-deep and stained watermelon red. All the
way out to Elkhart Park. Long days. Soaked socks. Skin raw
from wind and sun—and joy, too. That quiet, unspeakable
joy that comes from pushing far and not breaking.

Somewhere out there, between two unnamed lakes, I laid down in the grass and didn't move for an hour. Nothing happened.

That was the point.

All of it built on the backs of dozens of trips. Hundreds of days. Thousands of hours outside. And now? There's just one final stretch of trail I haven't touched—one last section between the headwaters and Sweetwater to tie it all together. One more piece of a world-renowned range that's become, over time, something like home.

Success hasn't always looked like the summit. Sometimes it's the weight of the pack. The silence at sunrise. The grin of someone who finally believed they could make it.

But leading others through it?
That's another level entirely.

Winter canyoneering descents in Zion—rappels down sandstone coated in ice, dropping into pools so cold it bites through the wetsuit, daylight short, margins thinner than usual. Or springtime slots in the San Rafael Swell, narrow and echoing, the sandstone warm against the palms, water frigid, angry clouds appearing overhead like magic, warning of impending doom. And caves—always caves—where the cold creeps into your bones, where light vanishes behind you and every sound is swallowed.

Every trip like that, most of the gear is mine. The ropes, the webbing, the carabiners—the weight of safety packed in coils and bags. The knowledge, too. Anchor placement, contingency systems, escape plans. The knots? Always mine. Tied, checked, tied again. Every step I speak aloud—not because they need to grasp every detail, but because they deserve to hear how trust is built. How you double-check your own work *and* still bring in a second set of eyes—because when lives hang from a system, yours aren't enough.

They *never* are.

And still—the fear, the challenge, the thrill, and that rare, rare awe—those are shared. Equally. I don't own those. Nobody does. You just open the door to it and walk through together.

People don't follow because you're fearless.
They follow because you've been scared and kept moving.
Because you fall and climb again—quietly.
Because you go first when it matters,
and stay when it's hard.

Leadership isn't a voice shouting from the front.
It's a rope, anchored well, that says:
This way's safe. You've got this.

There's a ritual to it now.
One that feels as essential as the trip itself.

I lay everything out—packs emptied, gear grouped like offerings to some ancient god of preparedness. Rope, ascenders, foot loops, cows tails, helmets, spare batteries, printed maps sealed in weatherproof sleeves. Don't forget the butt wipe. Camera charged, first aid stocked, 3 lamps per person. Meals are weighed and sealed with the precision of a backcountry pharmacist. There's a pile of gear for me, a pile for someone I'm taking, and a third pile for what someone joining didn't know they'd forget.

It's quiet work, careful and familiar. As my hands sort gear with practiced care, something restless in me settles. This is when I'm not proving anything. I'm preparing. It's its own kind of love—toward the people joining, the mountains I'll move through, and toward the version of myself I want to return.

Later, I crawl into bed beside her.

The same woman I once lost—and somehow found again. Not by retracing old steps, but by choosing a new path. The marriage ended. What we built after didn't have a name, but it had truth. And like a well-set anchor, it held.

She knows the rhythm now. She doesn't try to hold me back. She pulls the blankets higher around me and mutters: "Take a hike."

She means it. She means go.

Because she knows I come back better. Not
because I've conquered anything—but because
I've stayed sharp. Stayed honest. Stayed alive.

Because now, I don't disappear. I don't dim. I go—with
intention, with heart—and I come back as myself.

Sometimes staying alive means climbing
back out the same way you came in.

I clip into the rope and lean back, setting my
ascenders. Preparing to climb. Staring into the
nothing above, where the rope disappears into
darkness. One step up, three hundred to go.

Something deep in me braced,
like it had its own grip on the rope.

That's when it starts.

A low roar funnels down the shaft—then hail, slamming
through the entrance pit. We hear it ricochet off the
hourglass-shaped walls—pinging in the narrow middle
like a pinball—before it explodes into the chamber below.
It rushes down from the hidden rope top, smacking our
helmets with a force that makes us laugh like maniacs.

Hail. Underground.

Echoing like thunder inside a chest of stone.
A ceiling with no sky.

Then quiet—just rope and water and breath.
We climb through the void until the light changes.
Moss. Cold stone. Then sky.

At the surface the storm finds us again—
hail hammering as if it had been waiting.
We throw our arms up and howl, grinning like fools.

Later, when the echo fades,
I think about those hailstones—
how far they traveled,
how something small can fall
from the sky and still find you in the dark.
Not everything you leave behind stays where it's dropped.
Some things rise.
Changed, reshaped, still yours to carry differently.

You come prepared, and nature offers something back.
Sometimes.

That's the deal.
It always was.

BEFORE HAIL • Photograph

THE DIRECTION

Morning light cuts through spruce
branches as I shoulder my pack.

I used to think Leave No Trace was just
trailhead rules printed on a wooden sign.
Pack it in, pack it out.
Don't build fire rings. Bury your waste.
It was about being a good camper—
about keeping the wild, wild.

But somewhere along the way,
I realized it's more than that.
It's a way of living.

When I walk through the backcountry now,
I move with intention.
I notice how fragile things are—the moss that
takes years to grow, the alpine flower that
blooms once and never again that season.

I think about where I step, not just because of what's
underfoot, but because someone will come after me.
Someone always does.

And the same is true in life. In relationships.
In the spaces we share with each other.

It's easy to leave a mess when you're hurting.

I've done it. Emotionally. Physically. I've offloaded
what I couldn't carry—without consent, without
warning—onto people I loved. I've left others to
clean up what I wasn't strong enough to face.

But now I try to carry it out. I try to leave each
place—each person—a little better for having
passed through. Or at the very least, not worse.

Out there, I think twice before peeing uphill from
a stream. At home, I think twice before dumping
my frustration on a stranger, or letting my garbage
pile up in someone else's emotional backyard.

It's the same principle, really. You're never alone. Even
when it feels like it. The traces we leave ripple outward.

I still ask myself what I'm leaving behind. A broken
bottle at the edge of a lake, waiting for a bare foot—
or a story that might lighten someone's load. A burn
scar, or a sign that something bloomed here once.

Probably both. Hopefully more of one. I'm still learning.
Still a collection of messy parts. But I'm watching my
footprints more closely these days, because I know
now how long it takes for some places to heal.

My father was Conscience. Question. Compass.
My mother—less a voice than a presence.
Felt in the hush after hail,
in the shimmer of quaking aspen leaves,
the quiet way earth bears weight
and still offers green.

One taught me to ask the hard questions.
The other taught me how to hold the answers gently.

And love—real love—asks neither for masks nor shrinking.
It pulls the blanket higher and says, "Go."

I still hear the question sometimes.
But it doesn't sting like it used to.
It doesn't accuse.
It invites.
There's an eagerness to it now—
a sense of something waiting.

And though it's no longer in his voice,
I can still picture his face—
lit up and curious—
as he looked up from those photos
of the Colorado River.

What now?

AUTHOR NOTE

I didn't write this to explain everything.
I wrote it to listen — to the echoes, to the dark,
to the parts I tried to leave behind.

If any of it rang true, thank you for staying with it.

This was one descent.
There's more to come…
above ground, on the line, and deeper still.

The work will keep changing forms.
But it will keep listening.

YOU'RE NOT ALONE ON THE ROPE

Resources for Recovery, Clarity, and Safety

Mental Health & Crisis Support

- 988 Suicide & Crisis Lifeline — Call or text 988

- NAMI (National Alliance on Mental Illness) — www.nami.org

- SAMHSA National Helpline — 1-800-662-HELP (4357)

- Mental Health America — www.mhanational.org

Substance Use & Addiction Support

- Alcoholics Anonymous — 24/7 Helpline 1-800-839-1686

- SMART Recovery — Science-based support groups (www.smartrecovery.org)

Outdoor & Safety Organizations

- National Speleological Society (NSS) — www.caves.org

- American Mountain Guides Association (AMGA) — www.amga.com

- Leave No Trace — www.lnt.org

- The American Alpine Club — www.americanalpineclub.org

(Phone numbers and web addresses current at time of publication.)